THE TRUE COST OF FASHION

How to Shop to Change the World

Louise Spilsbury

WAYLAND

Published in paperback in 2014 by Wayland
Copyright © Wayland 2014

Wayland
338 Euston Road
London NW1 3BH

Wayland Australia
Level 17/207 Kent Street
Sydney. NSW 2000

Produced for Wayland by Calcium
Design concept by Lisa Peacock

Picture acknowledgements
Dreamstime: Casadphoto 33t, Dleonis 31b, Federicofoto 34, Gopixgo 32, Hupeng 2, 18t, Josefhanus 35, Joycemlheureux 23t, Vadim Kulikov 36b, Logit 7t, Jennifer Pitiquen 45r, Neil Speers 25t, Srki66 15b, Timhesterphotography 30, Ali Rıza Yıldız 33b; NatureWorks LLC: 41l, 41r; People Tree: 38, 39t, 39b; Shutterstock: Africa Studio 27t, Ustyuzhanin Andrey Anatolyevitch 26b, Ariwasabi 42, Bullet74 11b, Lucian Coman 15t, Songquan Deng 6t, Oguz Dikbakan 13bg, Pierre-Jean Durieu 45l, Leo Francini 6b, Gkuna 7m, Luisa Fernanda Gonzalez 11m, Homeros 23b, IMG_191 LLC 25b, Jtoddpope 28, Ragne Kabanova 18b, Ligak 40, Lindasj 22, 31t, Monkey Business Images 37, Mopic 24, Robert Naratham 29t, Nejron Photo 44r, OlegD 20, Edyta Pawlowska 9b, Tanawat Pontchour 17t, Lizette Potgieter 12, 19, Paul Prescott 5, 8, 14, 22, Rehan Qureshi 4b, Christina Richards 43, JeremyRichards 13b, Silentwings 29b, Silver-John 21t, Spirit of America 21b, StockLite 10, 44l, Svetlovskiy 6-7, Dennis van de Water 26t, Miro Vrlik Photography 9t, Waranon 17b; Veja: 16, 17m.

A catalogue record for this book is available from the British Library.

ISBN: 978 0 7502 8346 5
Printed in China
10 9 8 7 6 5 4 3 2 1

Wayland is a division of Hachette Children's Books,
an Hachette UK company.

www.hachette.co.uk

CONTENTS

FASHION CONSUMERS

Have you ever bought clothes from a supermarket or bargain **retailer** and wondered how they can sell them so cheaply? When you shop for a new outfit, do you think about who made it, how old they are, where they live, what they earn or what conditions they were working in? What do you do with the clothes when you've finished with them? Do you ever wonder what impact making and having so many clothes has on our planet?

We are all consumers of fashion. Every time we buy a garment, whether it's a high-fashion dress or a standard sports kit, we become part of the global garment industry. Millions of workers around the world grow or collect the raw materials needed to make clothes. Millions of others prepare and put the raw materials together. Some dye and cut cloth, others sew seams, make buttonholes, insert zips, and finish off by cutting threads and sewing on labels. More workers pack and transport the finished garments to the shops where we buy them.

The clothes you choose to buy, where you buy them from, and the amount of money you choose to spend, has an impact on other people in other parts of the world.

There are many stages in garment production, including making and preparing fabric. These rolls of denim are being finished before they are cut to make jeans.

4

Working conditions

Garment workers have to do their jobs in a range of conditions. Some work alongside hundreds of others in huge factories. Others are based in small workshops alongside just a few other employees, or alone at home. Some work in safe, comfortable conditions and are fairly paid. Others are ill-treated, badly paid and risk getting sacked if they complain. If you knew that an outfit was made by workers in a factory with no rights or poor working conditions, would you still buy it?

SUPPLY AND DEMAND

Around 8 million people in the world work in the clothing industry, but no one knows exactly how many there are. This is because many garment workers work at home or are on casual **contracts** – this means they are not listed as company employees so aren't counted in government statistics.

People power

In this book, we're going to look at what it means to be part of a consumer nation. It will explore where the clothes we purchase come from and how the **supply chain** (the route products take from the source to the consumer) works, from resource extraction to production, consumption and disposal. It will also look at the increasing number of examples of **ethical** practices, and the companies and organisations who work to improve conditions for people and communities and minimise impacts on the environment. What is the true cost of fashion?

Would you still buy a particular garment if you knew it was made by a young person working in poor conditions and deprived of an education?

SHOP TO CHANGE THE WORLD

Look at the labels on clothes hanging in your wardrobe and filling your drawers. Where do they come from? How much did they cost? Do you wear them all? How many clothes do you have that you hardly wear? Could you do without them?

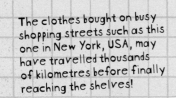

The clothes bought on busy shopping streets such as this one in New York, USA, may have travelled thousands of kilometres before finally reaching the shelves!

Top Ten Clothing Exporters 2008 Values in $US Billions		
Country/Region	Value	%
World	361.9	
China	120.0	33.2
EU-27	112.4	31.1
Turkey	13.6	3.8
Bangladesh	10.9	3.0
India	10.9	3.0
Vietnam	9.0	2.5
Indonesia	6.3	1.7
Mexico	4.9	1.4
USA	4.4	1.2
Thailand	4.2	1.2

Drilling for oil is costly and the Earth's supplies are running out. Some companies recycle waste products, such as plastic bottles and make them into new clothing, such as fleece jackets

Many garments sold by the fashion industry are made in huge factories with row upon row of sewing machines, such as this one in China. They are then transported to the countries they are sold in.

Raw materials are grown and processed around the world and transported to garment factories. Much of the world's cotton is grown in Bangladesh.

Top Ten Clothing Importers 2008
Values in $US Billions

Country/Region	Value	%
World	375.6	
EU-27	177.7	47.3
United States	82.5	22.0
Japan	25.9	6.9
Russian Federation	21.4	5.7
Canada	8.5	2.3
Switzerland	5.8	1.5
United Arab Emirates	5.5	1.5
Australia	4.3	1.1
South Korea	4.2	1.1
Norway	2.7	0.7

Source: (WTO, 2010), Apparel represented by SITC Code 84

CHAPTER 1

A GLOBAL INDUSTRY

The garment industry is one of the oldest and biggest industries in the world. It produces a vast range of clothing, from expensive designer fashion to high street and low-cost fashion, which often includes cheap copies of designer outfits. The industry also makes uniforms, safety gear, sportswear and fancy dress costumes.

SUPPLY AND DEMAND

The USA is the world's largest single importer of garments. As much as 97 % of clothing sold in the USA is made outside the country, in countries such as China, India and the Philippines. In the UK, 90 % of garments are imported.

An export industry

Fashion is an **export** industry. In general, most clothes are made in certain parts of the world and exported, or taken and sold, to other countries. In 2013, people spent around US$1.2 trillion on clothes worldwide. Most of the people who bought these clothes live in more economically developed countries (MEDCs): over one third in North America. However, most of the world's clothing is made in Asia – in China, India and less economically developed countries (LEDCs) such as Bangladesh, Indonesia and the Philippines.

Business opportunities?

There are positive aspects to sourcing clothes from around the world. Fashion industries often don't require expensive technology and skilled workers, so garment factories can be set up in LEDCs. This brings money into the country, which can help to reduce poverty. As fashion is a **labour-intensive** industry, requiring lots of workers, it also provides work for many people who might otherwise struggle to find employment. For example, in Bangladesh 70 % of gross domestic product (GDP) - the value of all goods and services produced within a country - comes from the fashion industry.

However, this is not always an equal exchange. The huge companies at the top of the supply chain might choose or threaten to move their orders from one country to another where, for example, wages are lower, so their profits will be higher. The companies at the top of the supply chain have a lot of power over smaller companies in LEDCs, who need to please them in order to keep their business.

Designer fashion is at the top end of the industry, where people may spend thousands on a single item they see on a catwalk.

CONSUMER NATION

The reason most clothes are made in LEDCs is to keep costs and prices down for the consumers. Do you think we expect to pay too little for our clothes? Do the people who shop in bargain retailers do so because that's the only way they can afford to dress themselves, or do they just like buying more clothes for very little money?

Lots of people want to keep up with changing fashions, so high street stores usually sell copies of catwalk fashion at low prices.

HOW THE SUPPLY CHAIN WORKS

The route that clothing products take from the source to the consumer is complicated. Many companies are involved, working across continents. At the top of the supply chain for most of the world's clothes are just 20 big, powerful **transnational** companies. Although these companies employ other businesses across the world, they usually base their headquarters in the USA and Western Europe.

Subcontracting

The transnational companies place orders with other suppliers and businesses around the world to source the raw materials needed to make their garments. This is called **subcontracting**. These subcontractors usually subcontract work to other, smaller companies, who in turn subcontract again.

Then the finished garments are transported to retailers (shops) to be sold. The result is that many workers in different factories and units around the world make clothes for one company at the top of the supply chain, that sells the garments as its own.

Companies at the top of the supply chain organise suppliers across the world to make and deliver garments with their company's brand name on them.

Who profits?

When a transnational company needs a subcontractor to make its garments, it creates a contract. This specifies the number, type and quality of garments to be made, the deadline for delivery and the maximum price per garment. To keep prices down and profits high, the company may encourage different subcontractors to compete for the job, and choose the cheapest.

To cut their costs, subcontractors may subcontract out to factories known as **sweatshops** that, for example, pay very low wages and make staff work long hours. Although these workers at the bottom of the supply chain actually make the garments, they might earn only **1 %** of their retail value. The company at the top of the chain takes around **50 %** of the garment's value.

SUPPLY AND DEMAND

A transnational clothing, textiles and footwear company based in the USA might use as many as 60,000 main subcontractors around the world, who each use about five or six subcontractors. So the global company has almost half a million suppliers!

Organisations campaigning against poor working conditions against some sportswear have accused some sportswear companies of using sweatshops.

CONSUMER NATION

When a transnational company is accused of selling goods produced by a sweatshop, it often stops doing business with that factory. Is this the right thing to do? Some sweatshop workers may lose their jobs and the working conditions may not improve when that factory wins a new contract. Could or should transnationals work with problem factories to encourage them to improve their conditions?

Sweatshop labourers are unfairly treated, but they need their jobs, so what can be done to improve their working conditions?

RAW MATERIALS

From fabrics and thread to metal zips, the clothes we wear are made from a wide variety of materials. Some materials are natural and come from plants or animals. These include cotton from cotton plants, rubber from tropical trees, wool from sheep and silk spun by silkworms. Other materials are **synthetic** or man-made. For example, the polyester fabric used to make many football shirts and the plastic used to make most buttons, are both made using chemical substances from oil found underground.

Cotton growers

The clothes that most people wear are made from either cotton or polyester, or a mixture of the two. Most cotton is made in China, the USA, India, Pakistan, Uzbekistan, Brazil and Turkey. The leading producer of cotton is China and overall, two-thirds of all cotton fabric is produced in LEDCs.

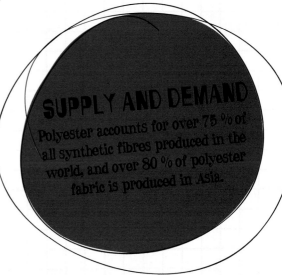

SUPPLY AND DEMAND

Polyester accounts for over 75 % of all synthetic fibres produced in the world, and over 80 % of polyester fabric is produced in Asia.

Picking cotton is labour-intensive work but poorly paid, so children are often asked to help collect it.

Producing fabric

There are important reasons why most fabrics and raw materials are produced in LEDCs. One is that some environments are more suited to growing crops than others. For example, cotton grows best in places with long, hot summers and heavy rainfall, and many countries with this type of climate are LEDCs.

Another reason is that it is cheaper to make fabrics in LEDCs. On average, workers in LEDCs are paid much less per hour than for equivalent jobs in MEDCs. For example, it is time consuming picking the fluffy balls of cotton fibres from cotton plants by hand. Often in poorer countries, there are fewer restrictions on young people working long hours. For example, for two-and-a-half months each year, classrooms empty in Uzbekistan because children take part in the cotton harvest to help their families.

CONSUMER NATION

When you pick up a cheap piece of cotton clothing, ask yourself how it was made for such a small price. Think of the hours involved in preparing the soil, planting the seeds, and harvesting the cotton plants, let alone the work to make the garment, such as adding finishing touches by hand. In Chapter 4, we look at some ways we can help to improve the pay and conditions of these workers.

Handiwork such as sewing sequins to a shawl, takes hours. Shouldn't people be paid a fair wage for such skilled work?

THE RISE OF SWEATSHOPS

When fabric has been made, it is transported to other workers, sometimes in other countries, to be dyed, cut and sewn into clothes. Almost 75 % of the workers who make the world's clothing are in LEDCs.

Sweatshops are workplaces where workers are employed for long hours, under poor working conditions and for low wages. The word was first used in Britain in the nineteenth century to describe the cramped, hot rooms where people made items such as shoes, clothes or furniture and were paid a **piece rate**. This means getting paid by the number of items completed, rather than the time it took to make them. During the **Industrial Revolution**, many factories had sweatshop conditions. Workers were ill-treated and risked injury on dangerous machinery. Today, working conditions remain very poor in many LEDC garment factories.

SUPPLY AND DEMAND

According to the American Department of Labor, over 50% of US garment factories are sweatshops.

Many workers in modern sweatshops are paid piece rates, too, so if they hope to earn a decent wage, they have to work very hard for shifts of **14** hours or more each day.

This clothing factory in Africa is well lit and spacious, but some workers in the textile industry face long hours and poor working conditions.

A worldwide problem

Sweatshops are not only found in LEDCs. There are sweatshops wherever there is poverty and unemployment that makes people desperate for work. In 2011, a television documentary exposed a sweatshop in Leicester in the UK, where Asian students worked in conditions that were dangerous, poorly ventilated, dirty and cramped, and workers were paid less than half the minimum wage. In the USA, according to the Department of Labor, over 50 % of garment factories are sweatshops because they break two or more basic labour laws, in places such as California, New York, Dallas, Miami and Atlanta.

£10.50

CONSUMER NATION

Are sweatshops necessary to keep costs down? Some business leaders say that improving pay would raise costs and that this would make consumers buy less and thus reduce the number of jobs available to poor people. However, given that wages only count for 1 to 5 % of the total retail price, if a worker's wages were doubled and the cost was passed on to consumers, the item would cost only 5 % more, so a £10 shirt would cost just £10.50. Would the higher price stop you buying it?

TRACKING TRAINERS

Veja is a small French company established in 2004. It makes trainers. The founders, Sébastien Kopp and François-Ghislain Morillon, set out to create a company that makes fashionable products with a conscience, from raw materials to sale. Veja get their raw materials from Brazil. By restricting the size of the supply chain for their products, it is easier for them to monitor their subcontractors. They can ensure that workers making their trainers are paid fair wages and given decent working conditions. They also keep better control of the quality of materials and manufacture.

The raw materials

The trainer tops are partly made from cotton canvas. The cotton is grown in Ceará in northeastern Brazil by small producers. Each grows around 150 kg of cotton bolls each year on a farm of around 1 hectare. The fibres from the bolls are weaved into canvas in the São Paulo State. Veja pay growers a stable price for the cotton for at least three years. This means that if one year has a poor harvest, or the world cotton price falls, farmers still get a fair wage.

Veja use cotton picked by workers who are paid a fair wage.

The rubber soles of the trainers come from the Amazon rainforest area of Brazil. Rubber tappers are farmers who cut into the bark of wild rubber trees in the rainforest to harvest the sap, which is called latex. They process the latex into rubber sheets from which the soles are cut. The farmers get a high price for their wild rubber, and this encourages many to preserve the rainforest rather than cut it down to sell wood, or to clear farmland for other crops or for rearing cattle.

Making and selling

The shoe designs are created at the Veja headquarters in Paris, France, but the trainers are made at a factory in Vale dos Sinos, South Brazil. Working conditions are good - workers earn more than the minimum wage for shoe workers in Brazil and have paid holidays. Once the shoes are completed, they are packed and transported by ship to Le Havre, France. Here, they are stored and sent out to shops by a centre run by Ateliers Sans Frontières. This charity finds work for people who have been long-term unemployed. At Ateliers Sans Frontières the trainers are received from Brazil and prepared for delivery to fashion and department shops all around the world.

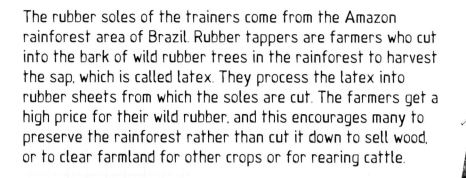

Tapping latex from a rubber tree to make soles for trainers.

The owners of Veja aim to control all stages of trainer production to ensure that workers growing and processing the materials used to make them, and the workers who sew them together, are treated and paid fairly.

Sheets of latex for trainer soles are left to dry.

17

CHAPTER

2

LABOUR BEHIND THE LABELS

The majority of garment workers around the world are female. In Bangladesh, for example, two-thirds to three-quarters of garment workers are women. In some places children work in the textile industry, too.

Women at work

Working in the garment industry is a positive thing for many women, especially those who move to towns from the countryside with no work experience. They need little training to learn how to operate a sewing machine, so can soon be earning a wage that can pay for food and lodging. Having their own money also gives these women independence and more freedom to make their own choices. Female homeworkers can also care for their children and look after the home in between work. However, there are problems, too.

Female workers in the fashion industry are not always given the rights that they are entitled to, such as fair pay and permanent contracts.

Female workers are usually paid even less than men. Some don't get **maternity benefit** and others are sacked if they become pregnant. They may have to leave their children without childcare, or travel a long way from their workplaces. Female workers are more likely to be cheated out of pay than men, and are more likely to be bullied or physically abused.

Child labour

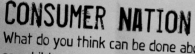

Many children work in the garment industry. This is usually because their families are poor and see no other choice than sending their children out to work. Many sweatshops employ children of ten years of age, or younger, who work around 16 hours a day. They use their small hands to do delicate handiwork such as hand-sewing sequins or beads onto tops. Although this type of child labour is illegal in most countries, it is believed to go on in many LEDCs, such as Bangladesh, Brazil, China and India. In fact, the **International Labour Organisation** estimates that 61 % of children in Asia are employed in sweatshops .

CONSUMER NATION

What do you think can be done about child labour? Some people say children should leave their job immediately, but that might mean they starve or are forced to do more dangerous work. Some say they should be put into care and their parents punished, but others say the solution is to prevent the need for children to work by making sure their parents have enough income.

Paying adult workers a fair wage should mean that their children won't have to work to help feed their family, too.

PAY AND CONDITIONS

Some businesses have taken steps to ensure that workers in their supply chains receive fair rates of pay. Many multinational companies say their wages are fair because they pay workers more than local businesses in LEDCs and the cost of living in these countries is cheaper than in MEDCs. However, many garment workers still live in poverty.

The cost of living

One problem is that even when laws state how much the minimum wage should be, this may still not cover a family's basic needs, such as food, shelter, fuel, clothing and education. In Bangladesh, Sri Lanka and Cambodia, for example, the legal minimum wage falls below the **United Nations** poverty line of US$2 per day, and most sweatshop workers earn as little as half of what they need.

When people are paid low wages, they cannot afford decent homes for their families, and may have to live in poor housing, such as here in Cambodia.

SUPPLY AND DEMAND

'Fast fashion' means people want quick access to cheap clothes, so workers are paid less. In Bangladesh, the **minimum wage** dropped to £7.16 a month by 2006, two and a half times less than its value of £18 in 1994. By contrast, the price of essential products such as rice, sugar, cooking oil and water increased by 200% in that time.

Sweatshop workers work long hours, often late into the night.

Workers' rights

The other problem is that many sweatshops ignore or abuse workers' **rights**. For example, Bangladeshi law says that workers should only work eight-hour shifts, but many people only get paid if they put in more hours (without **overtime** benefits) to meet unrealistic targets set by factory owners. Many workers are also on short-term (or no) contracts. Managers say they cannot employ full-time staff because work may be irregular, but having no contract

means workers have few rights or benefits, such as health insurance and holiday pay. This makes them cheaper than full-time workers and they can be fired easily if they complain.

In MEDCs, many garment workers are **immigrants**. In the USA, for example, there are garment workers from Latin America or Asia. Factory owners find it easier to exploit immigrants because they are unfamiliar with the area and the rights they might have.

SHOP TO CHANGE THE WORLD

Consumers can choose to buy clothes from companies that pay fair wages. Recently, international clothing retailer H&M signed up to the Fair Wage Network (FWN). This initiative helps to ensure decent pay levels for manufacturers around the world.

Many immigrants work in the garment industry in the USA.

HEALTH IMPACTS

Garment workers in some sweatshops and factories across the world face another difficulty. On top of low pay and long hours, many workers face unsafe, cramped and hazardous conditions, which often lead to injuries and factory fires.

Sweatshop dangers

Eye strain and injuries are common because some factories are badly lit or workers are not given safety glasses to wear when using equipment such as high-speed sewing machinery. Some factories have few openings to let fresh air in, so people working in dusty rooms, or with dyes and other chemicals, suffer from asthma and other breathing problems. There have been many fires in garment sweatshops, which are deadly because they spread quickly on floors filled with dry fabric and threads. Many workers also complain of constant fatigue, headaches and fevers, yet find it difficult to take time off due to illness because they fear they'll be sacked.

Women in factories often develop kidney problems because they try not to drink water during the day because they aren't allowed toilet breaks.

SUPPLY AND DEMAND

In 2012, around 250 garment workers perished in three factory fires in Pakistan and Russia. The employees were working in unsafe conditions in buildings where emergency exits were absent or locked, and workers were trapped.

A devastating fire at a garment factory.

Unions protect workers' rights and can negotiate with companies to improve pay and conditions. Sometimes, strikes are organised as a way of protest.

Improving safety

Campaigners say that a vitally important step is for companies to allow workers to join **unions**. Unions are organised groups formed to protect workers' rights and interests. Most workers are often too afraid of their employers and of losing their jobs to speak out against unsafe conditions. If they are members of a union, the union can support them if they speak out when safety regulations are ignored.

Some companies and unions are already working together to improve workers' safety. For example, in 2012, Phillips Van-Heusen (PVH), a major company that owns Tommy Hilfiger, Calvin Klein and other clothing brands, signed an agreement with unions to protect garment workers in Bangladesh from safety hazards.

SHOP TO CHANGE THE WORLD

How can we try to make sure that the people who make our clothes are treated fairly? You might write to companies to show you care about this issue, or carry out a survey to find out what other people think about these issues, and send it to retailers.

23

CASE STUDY 2
DEADLY DENIM

Jeans are incredibly popular garments worldwide – each year 5 billion pairs are produced, for a global population of just over 7 billion! Lots of people like their jeans to have a worn-in look and manufacturers use a variety of methods to make jeans look older, such as washing them with stones. One of the most widespread techniques used is sandblasting fabric, which means blowing sand fast at its surface to wear it away.

Life as a sandblaster

Most sandblasters work in poorly ventilated rooms in factories for many hours each day. They use hoses to sandblast areas of fabric they want to make look more worn, such as near the pockets and on the thighs. Silica dust from the flying sand fills the air and many workers have no proper breathing masks. The dust makes them cough and their eyes go red. They also breathe in many of the tiny particles, which then get buried into, and damage, lung tissue. This condition is called silicosis. Silicosis starts with shortness of breath but can progress to heart disease and difficulties with breathing and can even kill.

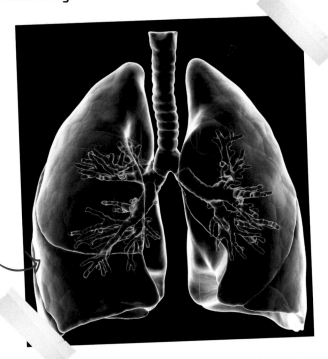

Sandblasting can damage workers' lungs.

Stopping hazardous sandblasting

Turkey was the first country to ban hazardous sandblasting in 2009 after over 40 long-term sandblasters had died. Turkey was encouraged to make the ban following a campaign by the Solidarity Committee of Sandblasting Labourers. Many of the worst sandblasting workshops were closed but the industry still employs around 15,000 people. Most of these operate safer, automated sandblasting machines wearing proper breathing masks in well-ventilated workshops.

But hazardous sandblasting continues in countries such as Bangladesh, Syria, Indonesia and countries in northern Africa. The Clean Clothes Campaign is an international organisation promoting safer work for people in the garment industry. One of its campaigns is to ban sandblasting completely. As part of this campaign, it lobbies fashion houses to stop selling sandblasted garments. By 2012, Levis, H&M and Gucci were amongst those that had banned the practice.

This worker is wearing a full safety mask while using a sandblasting hose.

SHOP TO CHANGE THE WORLD

It is possible to have worn jeans without hazardous sandblasting. One way is to buy second-hand jeans that someone else has worn in already. Another is to research information online and choose brands that have banned or are banning the practice.

3

ENVIRONMENTAL IMPACTS

The increase in the number of clothes people buy has consequences for the world's environment as well as its people. The clothes we wear, from the materials that make them to transportation and washing, can cause a great deal of damage.

Polyester is made from substances extracted at oil refineries such as this one.

Energy use

Fashion is an international industry in which most garments travel long distances in the supply chain, in vehicles that use a lot of fuel. Factories use huge amounts of electricity to power machines, and some energy is often wasted. The manufacture of polyester and other synthetic fabrics is energy-intensive and uses large amounts of crude oil, too. Oil and the coal burned to make electricity are **non-renewable** resources. This means they cannot be replaced and are gradually running out. Burning these fuels also releases gases into the air that contribute to **climate change**. This increase in the world's average temperatures can cause forest fires and is melting ice at the poles. Melting ice increases ocean levels and can cause flooding.

Ironing garments uses a vast amount of energy in the form of electricity.

SHOP TO CHANGE THE WORLD

The largest climate change impact from clothing is the energy wasted using washing machines, tumble-dryers and irons. You can reduce the environmental impact of one of your T-shirts by washing at 30 °C, rather than higher temperatures, and avoiding tumble-drying and ironing.

Waste

Another problem with low-cost fashion is the huge amount of waste it generates. Vast amounts of fabric are left over after patterns have been cut out and many clothes are thrown away after being worn only once, or not at all. This means the energy and resources used to make the clothes goes to waste, too. Most clothes that are thrown away end up in **landfill** sites. Some also pose a threat to local groundwater supplies. Fabrics such as nylon and polyester are not **biodegradable**. They do not break down in the soil. When it rains, water soaks up chemicals from these fibres as it drains through them.

SUPPLY AND DEMAND

In the UK, fast, cheap fashion counts for one-fifth of the clothing market. Over 1 million tonnes of clothing is consumed every year and about half of it ends up in landfill sites. Only half is collected for reuse or recycling.

Clothes that are thrown away and end up in landfill can cause environmental problems when chemicals and dyes seep out.

27

PESTICIDES AND OTHER CHEMICALS

Across the world, people use chemicals to help grow plants to make fabrics, and to dye, bleach or soften materials. Most of these chemicals do no damage and are very useful. They allow farmers to grow more productive plants, which help to keep prices down for consumers, and they help factories make useful clothes, such as crease-resistant shirts. However, some chemicals affect the environment where they are used, and the health and safety of the people who work with them.

The case of cotton

Cotton is easily damaged by insects and other pests, so farmers use **pesticides** to keep their crops healthy. They also use chemical **fertilisers** to help plants grow. Wildlife exposed to these chemicals can become ill or die. When these chemicals soak into soil, air and water used by people nearby, they can cause health issues such as lung problems and **cancer**. The chemicals are particularly dangerous for farmers in LEDCs, where workers using them are often too poor to protect themselves properly.

SUPPLY AND DEMAND
Each year, up to 77 million cotton workers around the world suffer from the effects of being poisoned by pesticides and other chemicals.

In some areas, cotton workers produce vast mountains of cotton so are exposed to large amounts of fertilisers and pesticides.

Dyes and finishes

Synthetic dyes and finishes can also be extremely harmful to dye workers. For example, some dyes contain chemicals that can cause cancer. Polycotton fabrics labelled as crease-resistant have often been treated with formaldehyde, which can cause a cancer called leukaemia if someone is exposed in high doses. Workers in LEDCs are at greater risk because they may have to use dangerous banned products or may not be given protective equipment.

Raw cotton is treated and dyed to make different types and colours of fabrics.

Many companies are taking action. Some dangerous dyes are banned and some companies, such as Bishopston Trading, use dyes approved by GOTS (Global Organic Textile Standard), which are safer, on their clothing. Today, more countries are bringing in health and safety rules to reduce health impacts.

Using natural dyes to colour cotton.

CONSUMER NATION

Are natural dyes better than synthetic dyes? What do you think?

Pros
1. They do not harm the workers like synthetic dyes
2. They do not pollute rivers, unlike waste dye from synthetic factories
3. They don't cause factory fires as chemical dyes have done

Cons
1. It's harder to get consistent colours with natural dyes
2. They are more expensive and difficult to apply
3. Making and using them requires the use of a lot of water and heat

CASE STUDY 3
GROWING ORGANIC COTTON

Patagonia clothing company promotes a healthy outdoor life using its products as part of its brand image. In 1991, its management team studied the environmental impact of producing the fibres for their garments. They expected polyester to have a major negative impact, but were surprised to find that cotton was just as bad.

A different way

By 1994, the company made a drastic change. They decided to stop using conventional cotton by 1996 and replace it with organic cotton. The differences between how the two types are produced are stark. For example, harvesting cotton bolls is easier when there are no leaves on the plant. Organic cotton farmers wait for low temperatures to naturally freeze and wilt the leaves. Conventional cotton farmers spray on chemicals to remove the leaves. They also spray on pesticides. Organic cotton farmers plant crops such as alfalfa next to the cotton fields. These attract ladybirds and assassin bugs that eat pests on the cotton plants. The downside is that organic farming requires more manual labour, increasing the price.

Cotton harvested from organically-grown cotton plants.

Risk and partners for change

Making the change was a risk for Patagonia because cotton represented one-fifth of the value of their sales each year. They found that organic cotton was scarce at first. This meant it cost three times more to buy than conventional cotton. Patagonia reduced their profits on cotton goods so customers did not have to pay too much more for organic. They worked to encourage more farmers and also other fashion companies, including Marks & Spencer and Timberland, to use more organic cotton, too. They believed that the public would also see the value of better cotton production and choose organic. Worldwide demand for organic cotton grew by approximately 10 % between 2012 and 2013.

Increasing amounts of cotton are being grown organically.

CONSUMER NATION

Do you think it is better to buy organic than conventional cotton? Look at the arguments to see which side you are on.

Pros

1. Reduces the quantity of agricultural chemicals in the environment and protects soil
2. Safer for cotton farmers to use
3. Cheaper for farmers to grow because pesticides are expensive

Cons

1. More expensive for consumers to buy, because of labour costs
2. Lower yield per hectare than conventional cotton
3. Even organically-grown cotton may then be treated and dyed with harmful chemicals

WATER ISSUES

Our planet may be covered in water, but most of it is salty seawater that we cannot use. Lack of fresh water is an urgent issue facing the world today as over 1 billion people do not have access to clean drinking water. The fashion industry has a huge impact on the world's water because it is the third largest user of water in the world, as well as being a polluter of water supplies.

Water for irrigation

Vast amounts of water are used by farmers to **irrigate** and grow fabrics for the fashion industry. Cotton farming is the biggest user of water, mainly because cotton plants are grown in some of the drier regions of the world. The Aral Sea, partly within Uzbekistan, was once the world's fourth largest body of fresh water. It has shrunk by almost three-quarters over the past few decades because water was diverted from two rivers that flowed into it, and taken to irrigate cotton fields.

Fish in the Aral Sea have died because the remaining water is too salty and polluted by pesticides. Thousands of people who depended on the Aral Sea for their livelihoods, and as a source of fish, have moved away as a result.

SUPPLY AND DEMAND
It takes an average of 8,500 litres of water to grow enough cotton to make just one pair of jeans, and 2,700 litres of water to make one cotton shirt.

Water use in factories

Large amounts of water are also used in factories that dye and treat fabrics. For example, to dye just one T-shirt uses between 16 and 20 litres of water. In factories making polyester, large amounts of water are also used for cooling machines. After dyeing, fabrics have to be washed, which also requires large amounts of water. When this is flushed away, it carries chemical dyes into rivers.

Rayon fabric is made from wood pulp from eucalyptus trees. Old established forests may be cut down to make room for eucalyptus trees, which require lots more water to grow.

Eucalyptus trees can be processed into Rayon fabric, but they require a lot more water to grow than the trees that they have replaced.

In the UK, 40% of a household's water is used for the laundry.

SHOP TO CHANGE THE WORLD

Most of the water used in the life of an average garment happens after it has been sold. Consumers use vast amounts of water to wash their clothes. You can reduce water use by washing clothes less. Check if something is really dirty before you throw it in the washing machine. Could it be worn again? You can also save water by only turning the washing machine on when it is full, to make the best use of water running through it.

4

MAKING A CHANGE

Fashion is an important global industry and millions of people rely on its success for their jobs, but it is also one that causes environmental and human problems. All around the world there are governments, people and organisations trying to find different solutions for some of these problems.

Governments and the fashion industry

Some people argue that governments of countries with major garment industries have a responsibility to protect their land and people by regulating how foreign companies operate there. Many countries already take action, such as fining textile growers and factories that pollute the environment, and encouraging trade unions to help uphold workers' rights. However, it may be hard for local governments to check up on all businesses and some will disobey rules in order to win contracts. Some people say it's the responsibility of world governments to make changes. For example, they could make trade agreements in which governments of consumer countries agree to ban imports of garments made using worker exploitation or environmental damage. However, other people question how these bans could be enforced.

Campaigning for change

Workers pinned up these shirts during a strike at a garment factory.

Some campaigners for change believe that government power over the huge transnational companies is limited. They believe that big brands and companies should use their power to ensure that working and environmental conditions in the global garment industry meet a high standard. Some organisations campaign for change by investigating supply chains of major garment companies and compiling reports about negative impacts. They report this information to the media to make consumers aware of the problems. Consumers can then use their influence, by targeting stores, for example, to encourage companies to make changes.

CONSUMER NATION

As fashion is a global industry, who should take responsibility for sweatshop conditions? Some companies say they cannot have any influence over laws in countries on the other side of the world and that it is impossible for them to monitor every contractor in their supply chains. Some campaigners say that if European and American companies decide what price they pay factories for products, they should also be able to push for the enforcement of their standards regardless of what local governments do. What do you think?

FAIRER TRADE

Some shops sell garments bearing a FAIRTRADE Mark. This means the cotton farmers have received a fair and stable price for their cotton. The farmers are also paid a Fairtrade premium. This is an extra sum to invest in various community projects, such as building a health centre or digging a village well. Fairtrade helps people to escape from poverty and to improve their communities for the future.

The organisation that checks up on supply chains and producers before awarding fairtrade marks is called Fairtrade International. It represents 24 organisations worldwide.

Fairtrade prices for cotton means fair wages for farmers, who can then choose to send their children to school and give them the start in life that most of us enjoy.

Today several companies sell Fairtrade cotton and fair trade school t-shirts, skirts and trousers.

Ethical trading

Ethical trading means improving the conditions for workers, not just getting a fair wage. The Ethical Trading Initiative (ETI) is an organisation that regulates and monitors working conditions. It has a code of minimum standards that companies are assessed on. These include providing safe and hygienic working conditions, banning child labour and working weeks of 48 hours or less.

SHOP TO CHANGE THE WORLD

In the UK, the school clothing market is worth about £1 billion and some of it is made from cotton harvested by children. There are ways you can encourage your school to buy from Fairtrade and ethically-traded sources. You could organise a Fairtrade cotton fashion show, perhaps in national Fairtrade Fortnight, to show people the quality and range of Fairtrade cotton clothes. You could inform others about the problem and organise a petition for change to present to the principal and governors of the school.

Members of ETI regularly check that their many suppliers and subcontractors are conforming to the code of standards. Critics of the ETI say that some factories are warned in advance about checks and that workers are instructed to lie about their real working conditions. However, ethical trading at its best both reassures consumers and helps workers.

CASE STUDY 4
PEOPLE TREE

People Tree is a clothing company that specialises in well-designed fashion garments. It also sells only Fairtrade and ethically-traded goods. The company was founded in Japan by Safia Minney in 1995, and launched in the UK six years later. Right from the start, Safia realised that her brand could only succeed in the long term if it produced garments that were on-trend, fashionable and desirable.

The company has promoted its brand in different ways. It has collaborated with many designers who are well-known in the fashion industry, such as Bora Aksu and Orla Kiely, and also developed designs endorsed by the film star Emma Watson. People Tree has over 100 stockists on the high street and online, its own store in Tokyo, and has shown its designs on the catwalk at London Fashion Week.

People used to think that Fairtrade clothing was dull and unfashionable but People Tree is one company that has helped to change this. People Tree sells clothes that are both fashionable and fair.

38

Promoting skills

People Tree's garments are made by small, skilled suppliers and subcontractors worldwide. For example, they employ knitters from Peru and Nepal, hand weavers from Bangladesh and jewellery makers from India. They encourage traditional skills and techniques, such as hand embroidery and weaving by featuring these techniques in their garments. They also pay fairly for the time it takes people to produce things such as hand-knitted jumpers and hats, not just as piecework.

People Tree pay fair wages to the craftspeople who make their knitted and embroidered garments by hand.

Slow and successful

People Tree is now a well-established brand. Safia Minney would like to open the brand's own stores in Europe but it is very expensive. She has said that she expected profitability to take many years. This is because the company acts partly like a charity with its suppliers. It helps them to build up their businesses. The company offers training, and helps them to set up their factories. It guarantees regular orders from suppliers and pays them half the money they will make in advance of producing the goods. This enables suppliers not only to invest in machinery and seed for crops, but also to pay wages to workers so they can send their children to school and feed their families. To help keep People Tree afloat financially while it develops its specialised supply chain, the company has borrowed money, but only from organisations that do not expect a very rapid return on their investment.

People Tree make clothes for men, women, children and young people in fabrics that last.

39

ECO-FASHION

Eco-fashion is clothing that is made in an environmentally-friendly way. This includes organic clothing, for example, but also recycled or 'upcycled' garments and those made with new types of fabric.

Recycling

Cotton can be recycled from old cotton clothing that is not good enough to be reused. It is shredded into fibres that are blended together, spun into threads and woven into new fabric. As waste is sorted by colour, recycled cotton does not need to be dyed with harsh chemicals and it does not use up the water and energy needed to grow, harvest and transport new cotton. Recycled polyester is made from used drinking bottles and old polyester clothes. These are shredded into small pieces, melted and made into new polyester fibres to make garments such as fleece jackets and board shorts. Recycling polyester reduces oil use and the amount of synthetic items releasing toxins in landfill sites and waste incinerators.

Merino wool needs less washing than most other fabrics as fibres trap fewer bacteria, which makes it good for performance clothing like running or mountain climbing vests.

Upcycling

Upcycling means reusing unwanted items by converting them into something better. In fashion, that means taking old clothes or waste fabric from garment manufacturing and stitching it into an entirely new item of clothing. An example of upcycling is turning a duvet cover or old curtains into a dress. Like recycling, upcycling reduces textile waste and saves raw materials, but some say it is even better because it requires less energy and resources to collect, sort and process unwanted items and waste.

Old and new fabrics

Companies are also developing new fabrics or sourcing more raw materials based on environmental considerations. Some eco-fabrics have been around for a long time but were little used until now. For example, hemp can be grown easily without chemical pesticides and blended with organic cotton or silk to make a useful fabric. Some eco-fabrics are completely new. Ingeo is a new fibre made using sugars extracted from corn plants. It has the useful qualities of polyester but it is the first synthetic fibre made from a **sustainable** resource (new corn plants can be grown every year) instead of oil.

Ingeo pellets made from sugars from corn plants are melted and spun into fibres to make clothes such as this T-shirt.

SHOP TO CHANGE THE WORLD

When you're buying clothes, look out for symbols on labels that tell you if a garment is made from organic or eco-friendly fabrics. Would you choose to buy them?

41

WHAT WE CAN DO

There is a lot that consumers can do to have an impact on the problems associated with the fashion industry. Some of these actions may seem small and insignificant, but if everyone does them they could and would make a real difference.

Slow fashion?

With fast fashion, people see clothes on the catwalk and want to be able to buy a cheap, high street version a few weeks later. Some people are shifting to slow fashion instead. This means buying fewer, better quality clothes that you wear more often and for longer. This slows the rate at which the fashion industry uses up limited resources and reduces its negative impacts on the environment. By paying more for clothes that take longer to make, companies are also more likely to employ workers full-time with fair pay.

CONSUMER NATION

Slow fashion is better than fast fashion. Do you agree?

Pros

1. Because you wear slow fashion more, its cost-per-wear is good value
2. By only buying what you need, you reduce waste and save resources
3. By paying a fair price for garments, workers are more likely to get a fair wage.

Cons

1. You won't be able to wear something new so often
2. Slow fashion is more expensive
3. Fashion won't be as much fun because styles won't change so often

Next time you go shopping, think about the purchases you make.

Reuse and recycle

Consumers can also reuse and recycle their clothes. One way to reuse clothes is to mend them when they get damaged rather than throwing them away. You could also learn to sew or ask someone who can sew to help you update a garment by reshaping it or adding new features to it. Some people reuse clothes by swapping them with friends.

Some people also choose to buy second-hand, or 'pre-loved', clothes from shops, charities or online services such as eBay. Buying second-hand clothes is cheaper than buying new, and often means purchasing something unusual that other people don't have. Buying or donating recycled clothes also reduces the amount of chemicals used to grow plants to make fabrics or dye them. It reduces oil and water use, and cuts down on the pollutants and greenhouse gases released into the environment from manufacturing processes.

SHOP TO CHANGE THE WORLD

Have a clothes-swapping party. Invite your friends round and swap clothes or give each other new ideas about how to wear the garments you already have.

There are many treasures to be found in pre-loved or pre-owned clothes stores or charity shops, and buying second-hand clothes is often cheaper and more interesting.

SHOP TO CHANGE THE WORLD

No one knows what the future of fashion will be. How will the industry react to climate change impacts, and shortages of cotton and other raw materials? In future, will people still be buying low-cost, fast fashion or buying less, and wearing more?

Under pressure

The world's population is growing and by 2050 it is estimated that there will be 9 billion people on the planet. Increasing populations will put increasing pressure on the world's resources and as LEDCs develop, the people in those countries will have more money to spend on things such as fashion.

With greater use of water and energy, climate change could make regions drier and resources in short supply. Natural resources would become more expensive, affecting the price of producing cotton and clothes, too. Increasing costs could mean there is more pressure on the environment and conditions for workers could get worse, too.

In future, will more of us buy cheap outfits that are worn only once or twice, without considering who made them or where they came from?

Hope for the future

There are alternatives. In future, consumers could insist that businesses show them their supply chains and that there are systems in place for checking worker conditions and environmental impacts. In future, people could be wearing more fabrics grown in a sustainable way, as well as new synthetic fabrics created from renewable resources. Scientists might develop new high-tech fabrics that absorb sweat to reduce the amount of times they have to be washed, or fabrics that last for a very long time so that people can buy less. Manufacturers could be making clothes in fabrics that are designed to be recycled into similar or equal products. Consumers of the future might be buying less not more, and buying high-quality, Fairtrade goods that last, whilst also ensuring the people who made them are given a fair wage.

CONSUMER NATION

Who has the power to change the future? Rich companies and transnationals? Sweatshop and factory owners? Governments? Consumers? Campaigners? Or do you think that all of these different groups have their role to play? Can all of us have an impact on the future of fashion?

Will more people become interested in ethical clothing in future and turn up to see fashion shows for ethical clothing such as this one?

Will all garment workers be paid a fair price for their work in future?

GLOSSARY

climate change   a change in the Earth's temperature and weather patterns due to human activity such as burning fossil fuels

ethical   morally correct

export   to send goods or services to another country for sale

fertiliser   a substance that is used to make the ground more suitable for growing plants

immigrant   a person who moves to a foreign country to live there permanently

importer   someone who brings goods or services into another country for sale

Industrial Revolution   the rapid development of industry in the early nineteenth century through the introduction of machines

International Labour Organisation   the United Nations agency dedicated to improving labour conditions and living standards throughout the world

irrigate   to supply water to land to help crops grow

labour-intensive   form of industry that requires a high proportion of workers

landfill   rubbish dump; site at which waste is buried under layers of soil

maternity benefit   a wage paid to female workers for a set amount of time after they have had a baby

minimum wage   a minimum amount of money set by the government of a country for people who work in that country to be paid

non-renewable   something that cannot be replaced by nature once it is used up

overtime   work done and paid for in addition to regular working hours and pay

pesticide   a chemical used to kill pests that damage crops

piece rate   work paid for according to the number of products turned out

retailer   a shop or business that sells goods usually made elsewhere

rights   powers that everyone is entitled to, such as the right to life

subcontracting   when a larger company employs a smaller business to do work for them

supply chain   the route products take from the source to the consumer

sustainable   when resource use meets present needs without harming future resource needs and supply

sweatshop   a factory or workshop where workers are paid very low wages for working long hours and under poor conditions

synthetic   a substance that is artificial or man-made, rather than taken from nature

transnational   giant companies that operate in countries all over the world

union   an organisation of employees formed to bargain with an employer

United Nations   international organisation of countries set up in 1945 to promote international peace, security and cooperation

FOR MORE INFORMATION

Books

Fashion (Behind The Scenes), Sarah Medina, Wayland, 2013

The Fashion Industry (Opposing Viewpoints), Roman Espejo, Greenhaven Press, 2010

The Fashion Industry (Global Industries Uncovered), Rosie Wilson, Wayland, 2009

Websites

Find out more about People Tree at:
www.peopletree.co.uk/content/26/about-us

Find out more about Bishopston Trading at:
www.bishopstontrading.co.uk

Read about where materials were grown or produced, where a garment was put together and distributed from at Patagonia's Footprint Chronicles page:
www.patagonia.com/eu/enGB/footprint/index.jsp

antenna.sciencemuseum.org.uk/trashfashion/home/wearwithoutwaste
Discover examples of environmentally friendly garments.

www.greenpeace.org
Check out this website and find out about environmental issues and what you can do to make a difference.

www.kidsforsavingearth.org
This website is all about how you can help to protect our planet.

INDEX